The Joy of Grandparenting

by Audrey Sherins & Joan Holleman

m Meadowbrook Press
Distributed by Simon & Schuster
New York

Library of Congress Cataloging-in-Publication Data
Sherins, Audrey.
The joy of grandparenting / by Audrey Sherins & Joan Holleman.
     p.   cm.
  1. Grandparents—Miscellanea. 2. Grandparent and child—Miscellanea.
  3. Grandparenting—Miscellanea. I. Holleman, Joan. II. Title.
HQ759.9.H65   1995
306.874'5—dc20   94-47541
                                  CIP

ISBN 0-88166-232-1

Simon & Schuster Ordering # 0-671-52699-5

Editor: Bruce Lansky
Editorial Coordinator: Craig Hansen
Photo Editor: David Tobey
Production Manager: Amy Unger
Desktop Publishing Manager: Patrick Gross
Electronic Prepress Manager: Erik Broberg
Cover Design: Erik Broberg/Amy Unger
Cover Photography: Bill Gale Photography, Minneapolis, MN

Published by Meadowbrook Press, 5451 Smetana Drive, Minnetonka,
MN 55343

BOOK TRADE DISTRIBUTION by Simon & Schuster,a division of
Simon and Schuster, Inc., 1230 Avenue of the Americas, New York, NY
10020

02 03 04 05   15 14 13 12 11 10

Printed in the United States of America

Acknowledgments

We would like to thank the individuals who served on a reading panel for this project: Cathy Broberg, Charles Ghigna, Babs Bell Hajdusiewicz, Karen Hammond, Jo S. Kittinger, Sydnie Meltzer Kleinhenz, Kim & Todd Koehler, Charlene Meltzer, Robin Michel, Lois Muehl, Claire Puneky, Robert Scotellaro, Nancy Sweetland, Esther Towns, and Penny Warner.

We would also like to thank the photographers who contributed to this book: pp. vi and 98 © 1994 by Kathy Sloane; p. 7 © 1995 by Bob Willoughby; p. 15 © 1994 by Joanne Leonard/Woodfin Camp; p. 23 © 1995 by David S. Strickler/The Picture Cube; pp. 31 and 71 © 1995 by Jeffrey Grosscup; p. 38 © 1995 by Elizabeth Harburg; p. 46 © by Jim Whitmer; pp. 55 and 87 © 1995 by H. Armstrong Roberts; p. 62 © 1995 by Marianne Gontarz/The Picture Cube; p. 78 © 1992 by Ulrike Welsch; p. 92 © 1983 by Ulrike Welsch; p. 104 © 1995 by Jane Jewell-Vitale.

Dedication

This book would not have been possible without our wonderful grandchildren, who have helped us discover the joys of grandparenting. Words are inadequate to describe the importance they have had in our lives from the moment they were born. We love and cherish each and every one of them.

Audrey's grandson is Maxwell Robbins.

Joan's grandchildren include Robert and Kate Doviak and Alia and Reza Mahmud.

We dedicate this effort also to our husbands, Richard Sherins and Bruce Holleman, who happily share with us the joy of grandparenting.

Introduction

What makes you coo in public, travel thousands of miles just to spend a weekend baby-sitting, weigh your wallet down with cute snapshots, and simply feel terrific?
A grandchild, of course!

The wonder of it all takes every new grandparent by surprise. No one is ever quite prepared for the overwhelming emotion that a newborn grandchild evokes. "Love at first sight" barely describes the experience.
As the years go on, the friendship that develops between grandchild and grandparent can enrich and reward both generations.

Whether you're a brand-new grandparent or a seasoned grandma or grandpa, we know you will identify with the sentiments we have tried to capture here. We hope that as you read this book you will smile and share with us the many joys of grandparenting.

Audrey Sherins

Audrey Sherins

Joan Holleman

Joan Holleman

The real miracle of life occurs
when your child's child is born.

A child is born only once,
but a grandparent is reborn with each
new grandchild.

❧

The joys of grandparenting grow
with every new addition.

❧

Life comes full circle
when grandchildren are born.

Now that you're a grandparent,
can you imagine not being one?

&

Grandchildren are better late
than never.

&

When your children give you
grandchildren, it's like having your cake
and eating it, too.

When you become a grandparent,
you really do feel grand!

❦

When you become a great-grandparent,
you feel both great and grand!

❦

Whether you're called Grandma, Gamma,
Nana, or Nama, or Grandpa, Papa, Poppy,
or Dampa—you'll love your grandchild's
special name for you.

When you have a grandchild,
suddenly every baby catches your eye.

❧

Can you believe how quickly your head
turns when a child—any child—
cries "Grandma"?

❧

A new grandchild is a magnet that draws
both sets of grandparents together.

Grandparents are as cozy as a second comforter. They add an extra layer of love.

Loving grandparents should be every
infant's welcoming committee into a
strange new world.

છ

Whether it's a single birth or quintuplets,
Grandma's extra pair of hands
can be a godsend.

છ

Holding a baby is like riding
a bicycle: once you've done it,
you never forget how.

Baby-sitting your grandchildren
is a labor of love; the only compensations
are hugs and kisses.

❧

When you baby-sit your grandchildren,
bring your running shoes and vitamins.

Grandchildren are treasures that can't be measured in dollars and cents.

❧

Grandchildren are the best prizes in the lottery of life.

❧

Before you had grandchildren, you couldn't have imagined how much joy they'd bring.

Every grandchild is extraordinary!
Ask any grandparent!

৪৯

Grandchildren exceed your wildest—
and your warmest—expectations.

৪৯

You don't think you could possibly love your
grandchildren more than you do today,
and then tomorrow comes.

Every grandchild is beautiful
in his own way.

෫ა

Grandchildren are like apples and oranges.
They can't—and shouldn't—be compared
to each other.

෫ა

Each new grandchild is a surprise
package—different from the
ones before and different from
the ones to follow.

It's easy to say "I love you"
to your grandchildren.

❦

Nothing says "I love you" like cookies
from Grandma's oven.

❦

The best way to love a grandchild
is unconditionally.

Your love is the best gift you can give your grandchildren. It's free, easily given, and easily returned.

Grandparenting is like falling in love.
If you haven't experienced it, you can't
imagine how fantastic it is.

≈

There's no price tag on a
grandparent's love.

≈

You can't spoil a grandchild with love.

Respect your child's role as the parent
and your child will respect your role
as the grandparent.

❧

Trust your children to be the best parents
they can. Look who taught them!

❧

It's important that your grandchildren know
how precious their parents are to you.

Before you criticize how your children are raising your grandchildren, remember what it was like to walk in their shoes.

৵৵

Parenting is on-the-job training. Allow your children to make their own mistakes, just as you did.

The first sounds your grandchild makes
are sweeter to your ears than your
favorite love song.

৯৯

If you thought your children made you
proud, wait until your grandchild
takes that first step.

৯৯

It's hard to believe that the tiny feet that
struggle to keep up with your long strides
will one day outrun you.

A grandparent's arms are the comfort zone
for a grandchild.

፠

You've got the whole world in your arms
when you hold your grandchild.

፠

A grandchild's arms around your neck are
like Velcro—snug, cozy, and secure.

A kiss is just a kiss, a hug is just a hug—
unless they're from your grandchild.

❧

Grandchildren are hugs about to happen.

❧

A grandmother's kiss can cure anything
from a bump on the head
to a broken heart.

The best face-lift is the smile your grandchild puts on your face.

A smile is the only way a baby can say
"I love you."

ૐ

You never forget how to smile
when you have grandchildren.

The sweetest words you'll ever hear are
"Grandma, I love you!"

❧

Small children often speak without
thinking, so when your grandchild says "I
love you," you know he means it.

Grandchildren love you just the way you
are—without makeup
or fancy clothes.

୫ଛ

When you love yourself, your
grandchildren's love will follow.

Grandchildren are proof that great things come in small packages.

℘

Grandchildren may be short in stature, but they're long on fun.

Having a grandchild around is a wonderful excuse for avoiding your work.

❧

Fun is always just around the corner when you have a grandchild.

❧

Lots of grandchildren in small doses is a sure cure for boredom.

Isn't your grandchild the cutest child
on the playground?

℘ə

You enjoy displaying your grandchildren's
artwork in your home almost as much as
your grandchildren enjoy seeing you
show it off to your friends.

You can't imagine how much more fun it can be to watch a baseball game than when you're cheering for your grandchild's team.

Children need grandparents, and grandparents need children.

ॐ

Grandparents and grandchildren are natural allies.

ॐ

No investments pay off like the bonds between you and your children and grandchildren.

To have a friend, be a friend. Cultivate your grandchild's friendship.

≈

You can learn as much from your grandchildren as they learn from you.

≈

Respect is a two-way street. If you respect your grandchildren, they will respect you.

Grandparents' photo albums are called
"brag books" for good reason.

ℛ

The reason grandmothers need
large purses is to hold all their
grandchildren's photos.

ℛ

Even before their grandchild is born,
grandparents show off its first photo—
a sonogram.

Grandparents can brag without
embarrassment . . . and usually do.

૪ൟ

No TV show entertains you the way a
video of your grandchildren does.

૪ൟ

As long as there are grandparents,
baby photographers will have customers.

A weekend alone with Grandma and Grandpa makes every grandchild feel special.

෯෨

You never get up on the wrong side of the bed when your grandchildren are sleeping over.

෯෨

You feel like a juggler in a three-ring circus when all your grandchildren visit at once.

Don't you wish you had your
grandchildren's energy?

❧

Grandparents don't need an afternoon at
the health club to get an aerobic workout.
An afternoon with their grandchildren
will do the trick.

❧

Grandchildren give you a shot in the arm—
even when you don't need it.

The good news is that grandchildren keep you young. The bad news is that afterwards you feel your age.

Grandparents love the excitement
of their grandchildren's visits.
Grandparents also love the peace and
quiet after the visits are over.

৪৯

Grandchildren are the fountain of youth.

Grandma's house is a home
away from home.

&

Even if the route is "over the freeway and
through the suburbs," Grandma's house is
still the best place for Thanksgiving.

&

Childhood memories of how Grandma's
house smelled and looked never leave you.

When you get together with your grandchildren, you don't have to "act your age." You can act their age and get away with it.

❧

All grandparents have a license to be silly.

Grandma and Grandpa have lifetime
passes to their grandchildren's world
of wonder and imagination.
They just need to take the time.

𝒴𝒶

Just a walk around the block
with your grandchild can open your eyes
to new worlds.

The best bonding between grandparent and grandchild doesn't shut out the rest of the world.

❧

Grandchildren are your passport to a world of fun and adventure.

❧

A grandchild can teach an "old" grandparent new tricks!

There's nothing like a grandchild's smile
to make you forget your worries.

🙢

Grandchildren light up your life.

🙢

Grandchildren bring sunshine
on a cloudy day.

A florist's fanciest bouquet can't compare with the bunch of dandelions picked for you by your grandchild.

Grandchildren can pick you up
when you're feeling down.

ℰ

Grandchildren help keep you flexible—
in more ways than one!

Grandchildren help you see the world
through rose-colored glasses.

៛ఎ

When you have grandchildren,
you look at life's cup as half full,
not half empty.

៛ఎ

Grandchildren give you a new lease on life,
with automatic renewals.

Neither rain nor snow nor clearance sales
can keep you from your grandchildren.

❦

A fear of flying can be overcome
when there's a grandchild
who lives 3,000 miles away.

❦

Isn't it great to visit your grandchildren?
Isn't it great to come home afterwards?

Grandchildren help you put a happy face
on life's little catastrophes.

❦

Grandchildren, like love,
make your world go round.

❦

Enthusiasm is contagious.
You catch it from your grandchildren.

No matter how many grandchildren
you have, each one has a special place
in your heart.

જી

When you count your grandchildren,
count your blessings.

When a new baby nudges your
grandchild out of the limelight,
create another stage for him.

৶৯

Grandparents always have enough kisses
and hugs to go around.

Giving equal time to all
your grandchildren is the ultimate
balancing act.

To keep up with your grandchildren,
keep up with the times.

❧

Grandparents need a life of their own,
just as their children and grandchildren do.

❧

Grandparents need to value their
grandchildren's independence as much as
they value their own.

Grandparents learn to expect
the unexpected.

❧

Overly generous grandparents can trip up
their grandchildren by placing too many
advantages at their feet.

❧

Grandparents need a sixth sense—
a sense of humor.

Show your grandchildren that you can
grow older without acting "old."

❧

You represent "old" to your
grandchildren—what a great incentive
to age gracefully.

❧

Grandparents can touch children's lives
in ways their parents cannot.

Grandparents are the solid roots
from which the family branches.

⚘

What a thrill to see your family's features
in your grandchildren.

⚘

Grandparents can start a chain reaction
of happiness in the family.

Although the past provides history
and the future provides hope, the present
is the time to celebrate family.

 familyɕ

Not so long ago, you showed your son how
to dribble the ball to the basket. Now he's
shooting hoops with your grandson.

Yesterday you sang your daughter to sleep. Today she croons the same sweet lullaby to your grandchild.

૪ཀ

The hand that rocked the cradle thirty years ago is the hand that now repaints that same cradle for the new grandchild.

If you thought your daughter wrapped you around her finger, wait until you have a granddaughter.

Grandparents get to have more of the fun
and less of the work than parents.

૪ઽ

Grandchildren are the bonuses for all the
work you did as parents.

A successful grandparent is one who is loved by his children and grandchildren.

જી

Having grandchildren doubles the pleasure of having children.

The "no return" policy doesn't apply to grandchildren. You can send them home when they get tired and fussy.

৪৯

Grandparents can enjoy, with their grandchildren, the things they didn't get to do with their children.

Grandparents may be forgetful,
but they always remember
their grandchildren.

℘

Grandparents need patience for all the
"whys?" of their three-year-old
grandchildren.

It's heart, not heredity,
that makes you a grandparent.

❧

You don't have to look like a
grandmother to be one.

❧

There's no mandatory retirement age
for grandparents.

Don't be afraid to show your affection
for each other when your grandchildren
are around.

୫ଚ

It's the ordinary things grandparents do
that make them so extraordinary.

୫ଚ

Never underestimate your ability
as a grandparent.

It's always "prime time" when you're with your grandchild.

There's no such thing as time
on your hands with a grandchild around.

୫ଚ

Time flies when you're with your
grandchildren. Make every moment count.

The quality of your life improves
when you spend quality time
with your grandchild.

૪ટ

There never seems to be enough time
to do all the things you want to do
with your grandchild.

૪ટ

Spending time with your grandchildren
is life's best preventive medicine.

The junk in your attic becomes treasure
when you share it with your grandchildren.

৪৯

Rediscover the joys of peanut-butter-and-
jelly sandwiches when you have lunch
with your grandchildren.

Write down your best recipes
for your grandchildren.
Let them help you prepare them.

৬৯

Grandchildren make the perfect audience
for your stories, jokes, and magic tricks.

৬৯

A grandchild is the perfect pretext to watch
Cinderella one more time.

Give your grandchildren a gift they are sure
to appreciate—your undivided attention.

❦

Don't be surprised if your young grandchild
likes the box better than the gift inside it.

A handmade fishing pole from Grandpa beats anything you can find in a fancy rod-and-reel shop.

ୡ

Grandmas are the reason children's boutiques stay in business.

Share the joy of reading with your grandchildren—as often as possible.

Introduce your grandchild to the books
you treasured as a child.

❧

Grandparents enjoy giving in to the plea
for "one more bedtime story."

Tend to your grandchild's bruised
feelings as carefully as you would
to his scraped knee.

❧

If you care about your children and your
grandchildren, they will know they are
worth caring about.

One interruption you'll never mind is a
phone call from a grandchild.
It rarely fails to put a smile on your face.

৪৯

A phone call from a grandchild
gives you something to talk about.

When you keep up with what's going on
in your grandchildren's lives, they will feel
comfortable sharing them with you.

❧

Keep in touch with your grandchildren—
wherever they are. Call, write,
and visit often.

❧

When you're a grandparent,
familiarity breeds content.

Some things need to be said,
to children as well as to grandchildren:

> - "I love you."
> - "I understand."
> - "I'll always be here for you."

8a

Some things are better left unsaid,
to children as well as to grandchildren:

> - "I told you so."
> - "Do as I say, not as I do."
> - "Can't you do better than that?"

Grandchildren of any age adore the
grandparent who is interested
in what they have to say.

☙

You can always find a good reason
to praise your grandchildren. Do it!

☙

Let your grandchildren know how much
they have enriched your life.

Grandparents' arms are long enough to stretch around all their grandchildren.

Secrets are safe with grandparents.

❦

Grandchildren say the darndest things!

❦

Hear your grandchildren. Learn to talk less and listen more.

Laugh at yourself. Teach your
grandchildren to laugh at themselves, too.

৯৯

When you're enjoying your life
to the fullest, your grandchild will catch
your enthusiasm.

৯৯

Your zest for life will rub off
on your grandchildren.

Children love to imitate—
so watch what you say and do.

ૹ

Children do as we do,
not necessarily as we say we do.

To keep the family history, pass it on.

౭౽

Let your grandchildren help you preserve old family customs. At the same time, welcome the new traditions that your children create with them.

౭౽

The bridges that grandparents build last for generations.

Introduce your grandchildren
to family traditions that will add
meaning to their lives.

Looking at old family photos
with your grandchildren unlocks treasured
memories for you and shows them
their special place in the family.

❦

Grandchildren love to hear stories
about their parents as children.

❦

Grandchildren love hearing your
"when I was your age" stories—
the first time.

The future belongs to our grandchildren,
but we can share the past with them.

૪ૐ

Who but grandparents can tell their
grandchildren about wringer washers,
World War II, and life before TV?

૪ૐ

Grandparents know almost everything.
At least their grandchildren think they do!

When you respect nature, there is more of it left for your grandchildren to enjoy.

୨୬

Introduce your grandchild to the beauty of sunrises and sunsets.

Encourage your grandchildren to follow
their dreams. Remember that you're never
too old to follow yours.

☙

A little advice from a grandparent
can go a long way.

If you believe in your grandchildren,
they will live up to your expectations.

Grandparents can be a safety net
when their grandchildren fall.

❧

Even when your grandchild drops the ball,
you'll still cheer her on.

❧

Help your grandchildren learn that a
problem is often an opportunity in disguise.

Images that last:
- the tiny hand in yours
- hugs that last forever
- *eyes that sparkle when you appear*

ℬ

Don't you wish you could bottle the
precious moments with your grandchildren
and save them forever?

ℬ

No matter what you put in your will,
the greatest inheritance is love.

Our children and grandchildren are the
message we send to the future.

৪৯

Grandchildren are our hope for the future.

৪৯

Once you have grandchildren,
you care more about the future.

Believe it yourself when you tell your
grandchildren that the best years
are still to come.

୫ஐ

Grandparents can see the future
in their grandchildren.

୫ஐ

Grandchildren are our legacy
for the future.

The time you spend with your grandchildren today gives them memories that will live on forever.

Also from Meadowbrook Press

✦ *52 Romantic Evenings*
Unlike other books that provide only a brief outline of ideas, this book provides everything a couple needs to know to create romantic evenings that will make their relationship come alive, with complete plans for a year's worth of romance-filled evenings, including where to go, what music to play, what to wear, eat, and drink, and more.

✦ *The Best Wedding Shower Book*
This revised edition offers valuable time-tested advice on how to plan and host the perfect wedding shower with great games, activities, decorations, gift ideas, and recipes.

✦ *The Joy of…Series*
Six treasuries of wise and warm advice for that special parent, grandparent, spouse, sister, or friend in your life. These collections reflect the wittiest and wisest (and sometimes most amusing) sentiments ever written about those whom we hold most dear. Each book is illustrated with black and white photographs that poignantly depict the unique relationships between family and friends. These books are the perfect gift to show a loved one how much you care. *The Joy of Cats, Joy of Friendship, Joy of Grandparenting, Joy of Marriage, Joy of Parenthood*, and *Joy of Sisters*.

✦ *Our Bundle of Joy*
A celebration of birth, featuring poignant poems, quotes, and stories written by the world's best writers, wits, and poets. Makes a great baby-shower or new-baby gift.

**We offer many more titles written to delight, inform, and entertain.
To order books with a credit card or browse our full
selection of titles, visit our web site at:**

www.meadowbrookpress.com

or call toll-free to place an order, request a free catalog, or ask a question:

1-800-338-2232

Meadowbrook Press • 5451 Smetana Drive • Minnetonka, MN • 55343